Art Director	Charles Matheson
Art Editor	Ben White
Editor	James McCarter
Illustrators	Chris Forsey
	Hayward Art Group
	Jim Robins

Designed and produced by
Aladdin Books Ltd
70 Old Compton Street
London W1

First published in
the United States in 1984 by
Franklin Watts
387 Park Avenue South
New York, NY 10016

Library of Congress
Catalog Card No: 83-51328

ISBN 531-04744-X

Printed in Belgium

Franklin Watts Science World

Geography

Dougal Dixon

Series Editor: Lionel Bender

FRANKLIN WATTS
New York · London · Toronto · Sydney

Introduction

Geography is the study of the Earth's surface. It looks at the size and distribution of the continents and oceans, and at the way different landscapes are formed. It also deals with people, studying where and why we live where we do.

This book begins with the changing surface of the Earth. New mountains are constantly being forced upward from beneath the Earth's crust as older ones are worn away by the action of wind, rain and frost.

But perhaps Earth is the wrong name for our planet: as we see in the section on oceans, more than two-thirds of the Earth is covered by water. Beneath the oceans are "landscapes" more dramatic than any seen on the continents.

Encircling the whole planet is another ocean – the ocean of atmosphere which makes it possible for life to exist on Earth. The Sun powers worldwide wind systems within the atmosphere that give rise to the many different climatic regions found on Earth.

The climate of an area is its overall weather pattern, which remains the same year after year. Weather is what happens from day to day. In temperate climates the weather is particularly variable, and we see how this stems from warm tropical winds meeting freezing winds from the poles.

The book ends by looking at the kinds of places people choose to settle in. Human beings change the landscape to suit their needs. As the book shows, some of these changes have brought great advantages, but others have seriously upset the delicate balance of nature.

Water is the great agent of change affecting the Earth's surface, whether it is the sea pounding away at cliffs, or rainwater wearing down mountains over thousands of years. Rainwater is carried in the atmosphere – the thin blanket of gases that surrounds the Earth – by vast currents of air. These air currents give rise to the different climatic zones on Earth, varying from the barren polar wastes to lush tropical jungles. Human beings have settled in all of these zones, in villages, towns and cities. Geography examines the effect we have had on the landscape around us.

Shaping the land

Atmosphere and weather

Contents

Geographical areas

Geography and people

Shaping the Land

Have you ever walked up in the hills and looked down on the valley below? The valley sides slope off into the river plain, which in turn stretches toward the horizon. On a really clear day you may be able to see for more than 50 km (31 miles). You might imagine that hundreds of years ago someone else stood in exactly the same spot and looked on almost exactly the same scene.

But it has not always been the same: thousands of years ago the whole landscape may have been under a sheet of ice hundreds of meters thick; millions of years before that it may have been covered by the ocean. The Earth's surface is in the grip of constant change. New rocks are created inside the Earth and are forced up to the surface to form new mountain ranges. Hills and mountains are slowly worn away over thousands of years by the process of erosion.

Erosion takes place everywhere on Earth. By far the greatest cause of erosion is the action of water on rocks. Water carries chemicals dissolved in it that soften rocks. This softening is the first stage of erosion, called weathering. Rainwater falling on hills runs into streams and rivers and these carry the weathered rock away. There are other forces of erosion: glaciers – huge sheets of ice – gouge huge valleys from the sides of mountains and wind-blown sand attacks rock faces. Millions of years in the future, your favorite hills will have been worn completely away by erosion.

▷ The view from the top of a mountain will show evidence of the processes that help to shape a landscape. The mountain itself is made of rock that formed millions of years ago. After this was pushed up from inside the Earth it began to be worn down. Rain and frost broke the rocks down into fine particles and boulders. Streams, rivers and glaciers made valleys in the uplands and spread soil over the distant plains. Finally, people came and built towns and cities, and laid out the fields and farmlands.

Key

U-shaped valley

River plain

Sea

Lake

Stream

The rock cycle

Hard rocks forced up from the Earth form the bare bones of any landscape. But mountain ranges are gradually worn away by the weather to become sand and mud, which are carried away by wind and rivers. These are deposited in thick layers of sediment from which new soft rock is formed.

New mountains forced up

Source of river

River plain

Sea

UPLIFT   Hard rock   Medium-hard rock   Soft rock

Erosion by River Water

Rain that falls on mountains forms streams and rivers. In their youthful stage these cut deep "V-shaped" valleys in the rock and carry away sand, pebbles and rocks. On flatter ground, the river slows down and stops cutting downward. Some eroded material is dropped here but most is still carried along. In its final stage, the river deposits great masses of the material as *alluvium*, which is laid down to build up the river plain.

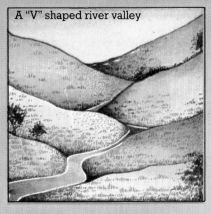
A "V" shaped river valley

A river valley in the youthful stage is "V" shaped

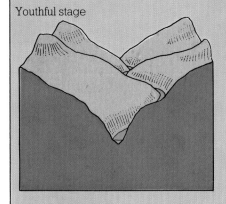
Youthful stage

Mature stage

Senile stage

Alluvium

Erosion by Glacier

Glaciers are found in very cold lands and in mountains. Huge sheets of ice, often hundreds of meters thick, glaciers grind out valleys with a distinctive "U" shape. They move very slowly – often just a few centimeters each year – but they can carry rocks weighing thousands of tonnes. When the glacier melts, it drops its rocky material in heaps called moraine. Small meltwater streams carry some of this moraine away. Large parts of North America and Europe are covered by moraine left by glaciers in the past.

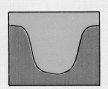
A glaciated valley is "U" shaped

Glacier

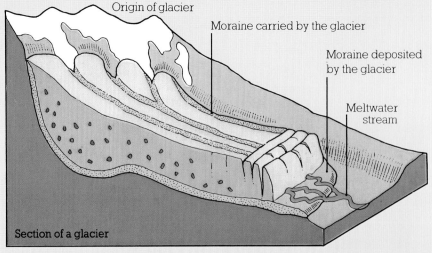
Origin of glacier

Moraine carried by the glacier

Moraine deposited by the glacier

Meltwater stream

Section of a glacier

Erosion by Rain

Soil consists of tiny particles of eroded rock covered with decayed materials from dead plants and animals. Because soil is comparatively light, it can easily be eroded by rain. The rain dislodges pieces of soil, which roll downhill. This is called soil creep and its effects are easily noticed. Roads crack as the soil beneath seeps away, and fences and walls lean downhill as their foundations are eroded. Trees have curved trunks as they try to grow straight after they begin to lean. *Terracettes* are bands of creeping soil held together by grass roots.

A moving hillside

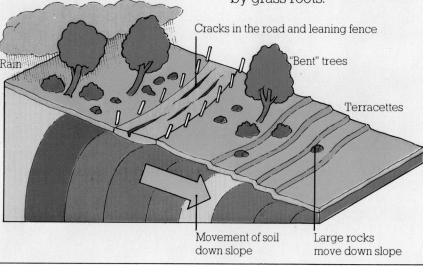

Rain

Cracks in the road and leaning fence

"Bent" trees

Terracettes

Movement of soil down slope

Large rocks move down slope

Erosion by Frost

When water freezes to ice it expands. This is what causes water pipes to crack in cold winters. A similar thing happens in nature. Rain-water collects in small cracks on rock sides. When it freezes, it pushes the sides of the crack apart, making the crack bigger. Eventually the freezing water causes the crack to fracture and the rock falls down the mountainside. This form of erosion is common in high mountains – in winter, in places such as the Alps or the Rocky Mountains, you can sometimes hear the sharp crack of the rock shattering. The broken rocks lie on the mountain slopes as piles of scree. Rocks that are eroded by frost in this way can be identified by their sharp, irregular outline.

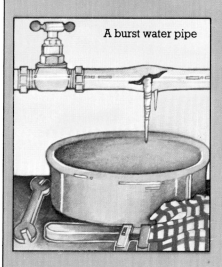

A burst water pipe

Water lying in a crack

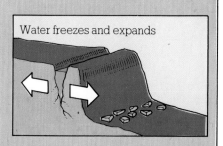

Water freezes and expands

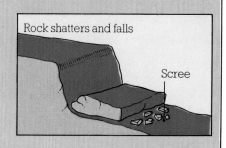

Rock shatters and falls

Scree

Erosion by Wind

Wind can erode rocks comparatively quickly in dry areas. Where there is little rain the soil particles cannot stick together and so they form sand. Wind blows this sand about with great force, and this flying sand wears away exposed rocks in deserts. You can feel the same effect when sand stings your face on a windy day at the beach. As desert rocks are worn down, they break up into more sand, increasing the amount in the desert.

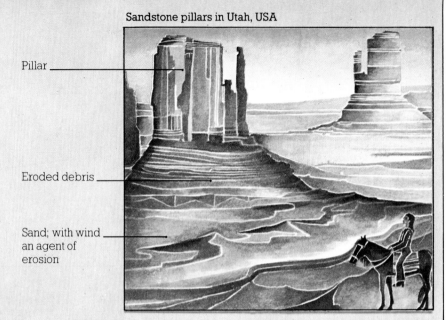
Sandstone pillars in Utah, USA

Pillar

Eroded debris

Sand; with wind an agent of erosion

Erosion by Groundwater

Stalactites and stalagmites

When rainwater seeps into the ground it is called groundwater. At a certain depth the soil and the rocks are thoroughly soaked. The top surface of this so-called "saturated zone" is called the water table. When the saturated zone and the water table reach the surface, as on a hillside, the water flows out in the form of a spring. In limestone areas, the minerals in the rock are dissolved in the weak acid of the rainwater. As a result the water hollows out caves and passages, especially along the level of the water table. Columns of limestone salts known as stalactites and stalagmites form in the caves. These are made of limestone minerals deposited from groundwater that drips from the cave roof. When the water table drops for any reason, a new cave system forms, leaving the original caves dry and empty.

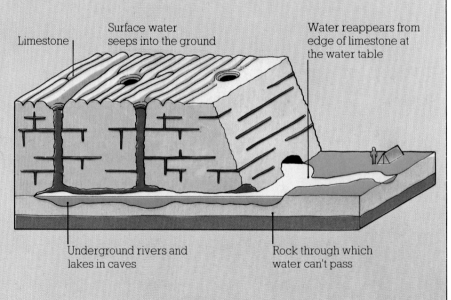

Limestone

Surface water seeps into the ground

Water reappears from edge of limestone at the water table

Underground rivers and lakes in caves

Rock through which water can't pass

Coastal Erosion and Transportation

Waves pounding away at cliffs eventually wear them away. Where the land is hilly, the valleys and hills will form bays and headlands. When the headlands are made of rocks of different hardness, they are eroded at different rates (1). As a wave approaches the headland it is swung around to hit the headland at the side (2). The headland becomes narrower and narrower until caves and arches are punched through it (3) and these collapse leaving sea stacks (4).

Coastal scenery

The formation of caves and stacks

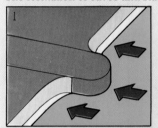

The sea erodes the soft rock faster.

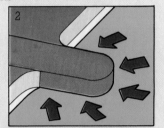

The sea currents swing around the headland.

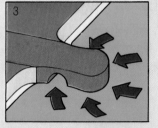

A cave is formed by the concentrated sea action.

The cave collapses leaving a stack.

Moving beaches of sand

Sand that is brought down to the sea by rivers is washed about by the sea currents and the waves. It is often heaped into underwater sandbanks which can be a danger to shipping. In other places it is washed up to form a sandy beach. Sand on a beach does not stay in the same place for long. Above the water it is blown into dunes by the wind. Along the shoreline, waves striking the shore at an angle wash the sand grains along the beach.

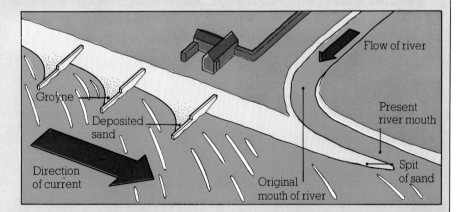

The grains then roll straight back down the slope. Sand carried along the shore forms spits at river mouths. Fences called groynes are built out from the shoreline to stop the beach from being washed away completely by local currents and tides.

Seas and Oceans

By far the greatest part of the Earth's surface – about 70 percent – is covered with water. If all the land areas on Earth were smoothed down to an even height, the entire globe would be covered by a layer of water averaging 2,500 m (8,200 ft) deep. More than any other feature on Earth, the oceans make it unique from all the other planets in the Solar System.

In reality there is one limitless ocean circling the Earth, but geographers have divided this into separate regions. By far the greatest ocean is the Pacific, which covers nearly a third of the Earth's surface. The Atlantic Ocean and the Indian Ocean combined occupy another third. Much of the Arctic Ocean, at the Earth's North pole, is permanently covered with a thick cap of ice.

Beneath the oceans there is a "landscape" of mountain ranges, deep gorges, plains and volcanoes. Sometimes these mountains are tall enough to break the surface, forming mid-ocean islands, such as Ascension Island in the Atlantic Ocean, or the Hawaiian Islands in the Pacific. Often these islands are the tips of volcanoes thrust up from the ocean bed.

Without this vast quantity of water, life would not be able to exist on Earth. The oceans are the source of all rainfall, and their currents help to circulate the heat of the Sun, keeping the planet at a moderate, fairly even temperature. And millions of years ago, it was in the Earth's oceans that life itself first began.

▷ The Earth's seas and oceans are constantly eroding the land at their shores. But new land can also be made – this coral reef is built up from the skeletons of billions of tiny sea creatures.

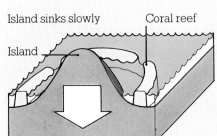

Island sinks slowly   Coral reef   The coral grows   Reef lagoon   Island submerged

Island

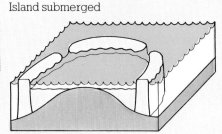

A coral atoll

Geological processes may force up a new volcanic island from the ocean floor, or existing islands may sink beneath the surface. The corals – tiny sea-creatures – use the island as a firm base to build upon to produce a fringing reef. Later animals build upon the earlier skeletons. As the island sinks a barrier reef is formed. When the island sinks completely the coral continues to grow, creating a ring shaped atoll. Corals are only able to grow in warm, clear water, so reefs are only found in tropical waters, away from the muddy river mouths of continents.

Land and water on Earth

The Earth is divided almost equally into land and ocean hemispheres. From a point high above the Pacific Ocean the only land you could see are the coastlines of North and South America and Asia and Australia. Above the land hemisphere, most of Asia, Africa and the northern parts of North America can be seen. But even in the land hemisphere there are almost equal areas of ocean and continent.

The proportion of land and sea

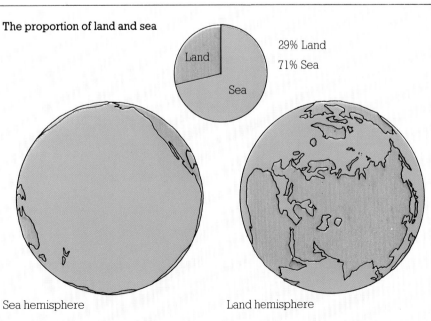

29% Land
71% Sea

Land

Sea

Sea hemisphere

Land hemisphere

Ocean Features

The ocean floor has a number of distinct levels. Close to a continent, and part of the continent itself, is the continental shelf. This slopes gently to a depth of about 130 m (394 ft). The shelf extends from about 70 km to 1,200 km (43 to 746 miles) from the shoreline, and then plunges dramatically down the steep continental slope and the gentler continental rise to the abyssal plain.

Continental shelf
The floor of the continental shelf is covered with sediments deposited by rivers. It is in this area that most fishing takes place.

Continental slope
The continental slope is cut by deep canyons. Sediments from the rivers and the continental shelf flow down these huge gorges.

Section of the ocean floor

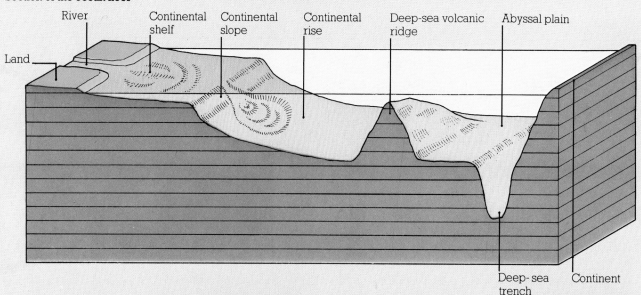

River — Continental shelf — Continental slope — Continental rise — Deep-sea volcanic ridge — Abyssal plain

Land

Deep-sea trench — Continent

The abyssal plain lies at a depth of about 4,000 m (13,120 ft), and takes up the greatest area of the ocean floor. Rising from the middle of the plain are steep ridges, often breaking the surface to form mid-ocean islands. At the edge of some continental shelves are deep sea trenches, their bottoms filled with thick layers of sediment, lying at a depth of some 11 km (6.8 miles).

Abyssal plain
The abyssal plain is covered with a slimy substance called ooze, made from the remains of dead animals and plants that sink slowly from above.

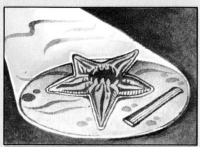

Ocean trenches
Even the deepest of these contain animal life. Worms and starfish live here in total darkness and under tremendous pressures.

Tides

Tides

At the seaside the tide goes in and out twice a day. Tides are caused by the pull of gravity of the Moon and the Sun, and the forces produced by the Earth's movement through space.

The tideline on a beach

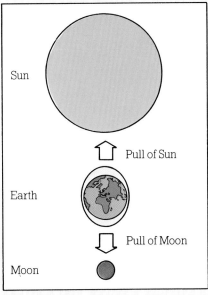

Sun

Pull of Sun

Earth

Pull of Moon

Moon

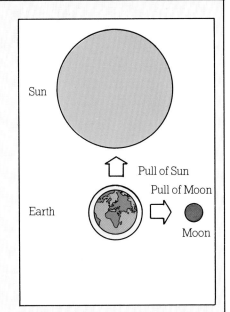

Sun

Pull of Sun

Pull of Moon

Earth

Moon

Spring tides

When the Earth, Moon and Sun are in line there are high high tides and low low tides.

Neap tides

One week later there are low high tides and high low tides as the gravity effects conflict.

Ocean Currents

Penguins on the Equator

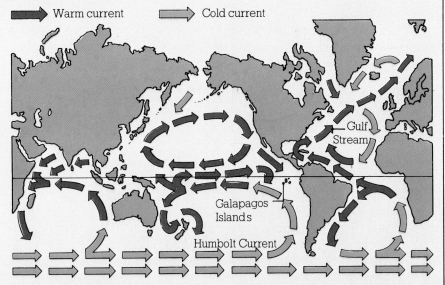

Warm current   Cold current

Gulf Stream

Galapagos Islands

Humbolt Current

The water of the Earth's oceans is constantly moving. Currents sweep warm water from the tropics north and south to the poles and bring cold water back to warmer zones. This helps to keep the Earth at a relatively even temperature. The warm Gulf Stream flows up past northern Europe. Because of this, tropical plants can grow on the south west coast of Britain, which would normally lie too far to the north. Penguins are found on the Galapagos Islands near the Equator in the Pacific Islands, where the cold Humboldt Current flows by. These currents flow on the ocean's surface; underneath, other currents may flow in an opposite direction.

The Atmosphere

The Earth is blanketed by a thin envelope of gases we call the atmosphere. It protects the Earth from the fierce heat of the Sun during the day and prevents heat escaping into space by night. The atmosphere consists mainly of the gases nitrogen and oxygen, but it also carries water vapor to all parts of the Earth.

Although it consists of gases, the atmosphere has weight and is held to the Earth by the pull of gravity. About 90 percent of all the atmosphere is contained in a layer between 8 to 16 km (5 to 10 miles) thick called the troposphere. It is in this zone that all forms of life occur and almost all weather effects take place. At a height of about 400 km (250 miles) the atmosphere fades away into the emptiness of space.

Weather and the climatic regions of the world are the result of movements of currents of air within the atmosphere. The powerhouse of these movements is the Sun. The Sun heats up the land and the ocean, and they in turn warm the air above them. But this heating effect is not evenly spread over the whole globe, so areas of warm and cold air are produced. The warm air rises and cold air floods in to fill its place, creating global wind patterns known as prevailing winds. These carry water evaporated from the sea which may fall as rain on continents thousands of kilometers away.

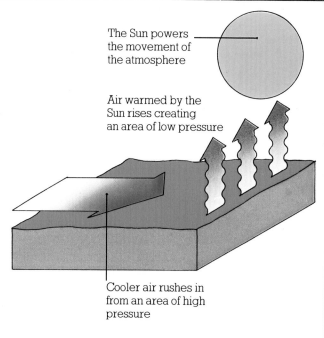

▷ Currents of rising warm air are known as thermals. Gliders use thermals to gain extra height. Because they have no engines, gliders depend on the prevailing winds in any given area. Seabirds often use thermals as they soar around cliffs.

Pressure zones

When air is heated by the Sun it expands. The same amount of air occupies a larger volume, so the air pressure beneath it – the air's "weight" – is less. So areas of rising air are called low pressure zones. Cooler air from zones of higher pressure floods in to replace the rising air. If this air comes from off the sea it may bring rain. Since no air flows into the zones of high pressure, these are often associated with periods of settled weather.

The Sun powers the movement of the atmosphere

Air warmed by the Sun rises creating an area of low pressure

Cooler air rushes in from an area of high pressure

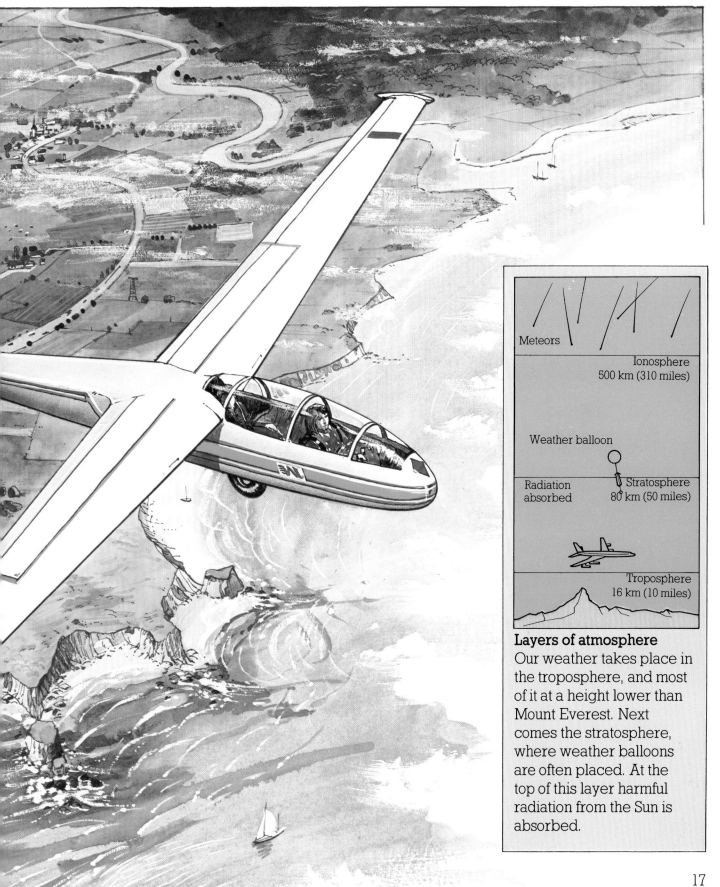

Meteors

Ionosphere
500 km (310 miles)

Weather balloon

Radiation
absorbed

Stratosphere
80 km (50 miles)

Troposphere
16 km (10 miles)

Layers of atmosphere
Our weather takes place in the troposphere, and most of it at a height lower than Mount Everest. Next comes the stratosphere, where weather balloons are often placed. At the top of this layer harmful radiation from the Sun is absorbed.

The Moving Atmosphere

A strong wind

At the equator, the Sun is always directly overhead, so here its heating effect is greatest. At the poles, the Sun's rays have to pass through a thicker layer of atmosphere and fall on a greater area of the Earth's surface, so here the heating effect is least. The result is that warm air rises at the equator, creating a low pressure zone. At the poles, cold air sinks and pushes outward. This gives rise to the world's prevailing winds. Trade Winds flow into the low pressure zone at the equator, while the Polar Easterlies are the masses of cold air pushing out from the poles. As the Easterlies move into warmer areas they heat up and rise, creating another zone of low pressure, which draws in the warm Westerlies from the tropics.

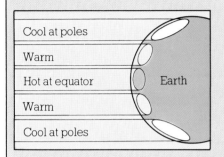

Cool at poles
Warm
Hot at equator — Earth
Warm
Cool at poles

The pressure zones

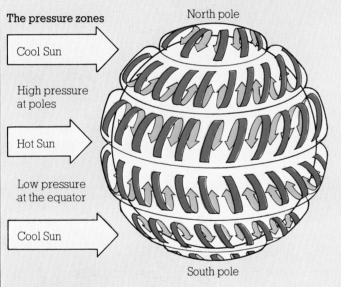

Cool Sun

High pressure at poles

Hot Sun

Low pressure at the equator

Cool Sun

North pole

South pole

World winds

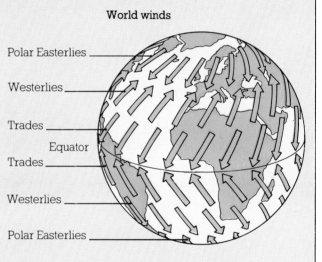

Polar Easterlies
Westerlies
Trades
Equator
Trades
Westerlies
Polar Easterlies

Onshore and offshore breezes

Local winds, as opposed to the prevailing winds, are caused by the heating of the land and sea. During the day the land heats up more quickly than the sea. The warm air over the land rises and the cold air from the sea rushes in, giving an onshore breeze. In the evening, the land cools more quickly than the sea and we get an offshore breeze from the land out to sea.

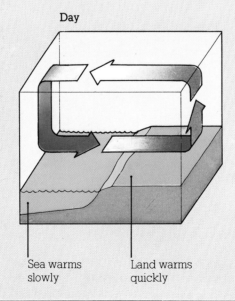

Day

Sea warms slowly
Land warms quickly

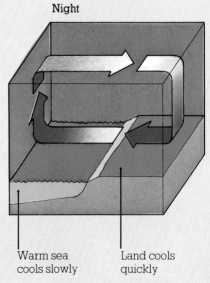

Night

Warm sea cools slowly
Land cools quickly

The Water Cycle

The water in the Earth's atmosphere and oceans is circulating all the time. The Sun's heat evaporates water from the ocean's surface and from lakes and rivers, and the moisture in the air can then be blown by prevailing winds over land. When the air temperature falls enough

the water vapor condenses as droplets and forms clouds. If the air becomes cooler still – when it rises over mountains, for example – the droplets become large drops and fall as rain. The rain collects in streams and rivers and is eventually returned to the sea, so completing the cycle.

Condensation on a window

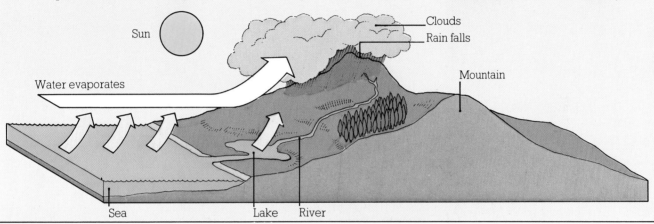

Sun

Clouds

Rain falls

Mountain

Water evaporates

Sea

Lake

River

Climatic Regions of the World

The world's prevailing winds and the rainfall they bring with them result in many areas of the world sharing similar climatic features. For example, there is a belt of thick tropical forest around the equator, and in roughly similar positions in the Northern and Southern hemispheres, deserts are found. Local features such as the presence of a range of mountains, or the closeness to the sea, modify the overall climatic pattern. The five regions shown here can be divided into smaller regions to show these variations.

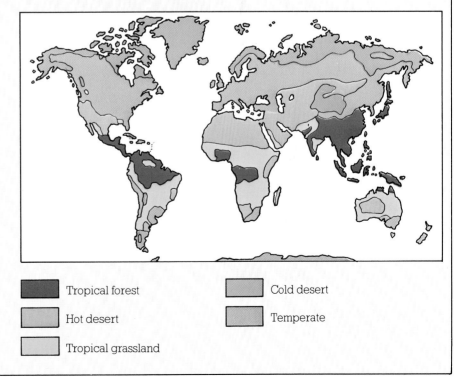

Tropical forest

Hot desert

Tropical grassland

Cold desert

Temperate

Tropical Forest

Along the equator, the rising hot air produces a zone where air pressure is always low. This draws in winds from the northeast and southeast called the Trade Winds. These winds usually contain a great deal of moisture. The air rises in the low pressure zone and drops its moisture as heavy rain. These conditions prevail throughout the year. The warmth and wetness give rise to thick tropical forests. The heavy rain produces large rivers in these areas, such as the Amazon in South America, the Zaire in Africa, and the Mekong in Asia.

Tropical forest

The Sun is hot and overhead, the land heats up, the air rises and drops rain

Wet prevailing wind from the sea

Hot Sun

River

Thick rich vegetation

Hot Desert

Along the tropics there are two bands of high pressure areas. These are produced as the hot air that has risen and dropped its rain at the equator cools down and descends. These dry winds spread out northward and southward. Since these winds bring no rain there is a desert belt here. The deserts of the northern belt include those of the south western United States and Mexico, the Sahara and Arabian Deserts and the Thar Desert in India. Southern deserts include the Atacama in South America, the Namib in Africa, and the deserts of Australia.

Desert

Dry prevailing winds descending from the upper atmosphere

Hot Sun with no rain

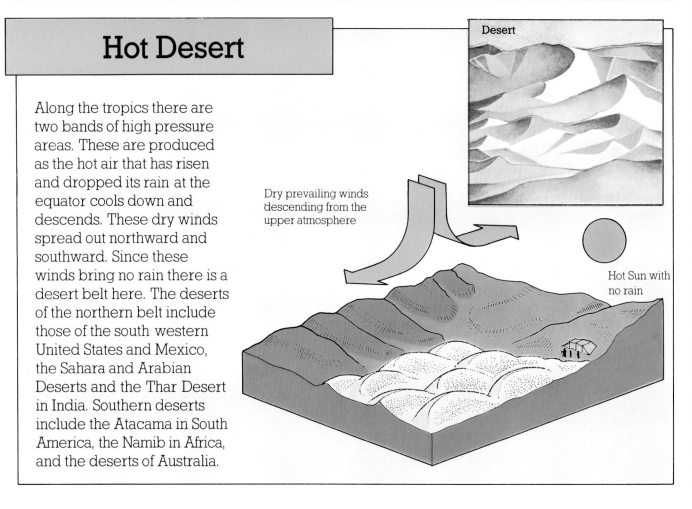

Tropical Grassland

Between the desert belt and the tropical forests there lies an area that varies between these two extremes. In the hot season, the Sun is overhead creating a low pressure zone that draws in wet winds. In the cooler season, a high pressure belt brings dry winds to this zone. This swing between wet and dry seasons gives rise to areas of grasslands. Grass grows well since it can survive the fires of the dry season, and there is not enough water all year round for trees to flourish. Animals here tend to come into the area only in the wet season.

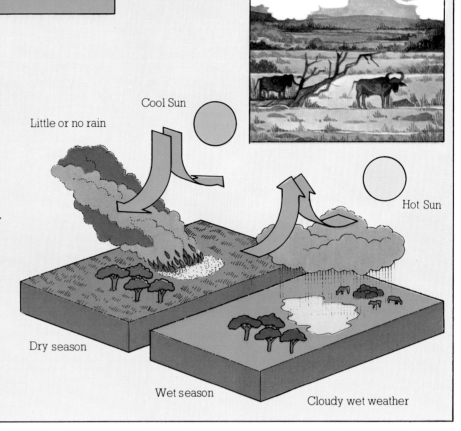

Tropical grassland

Cool Sun

Little or no rain

Hot Sun

Dry season

Wet season

Cloudy wet weather

Cold Desert

It is permanently cold over the North and South poles. Hence there is always a high pressure zone over these areas, with cold, dry air coming down and spreading out as freezing winds. The prevailing winds follow the same pattern as they do in hot desert regions such as the Sahara. Seas in this region tend to be frozen and there is always a layer of ice – called "permafrost" – below the surface of the soil, even in summer. Because of this layer, water cannot drain away. So in summer the landscape has lakes of melted snow.

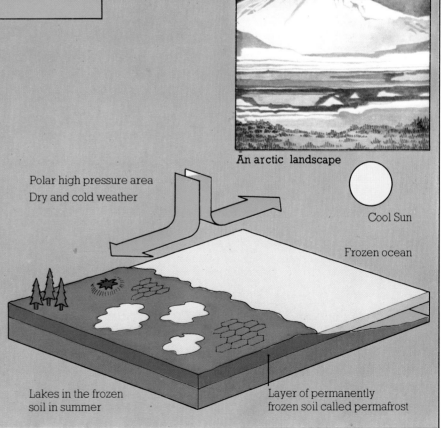

An arctic landscape

Polar high pressure area
Dry and cold weather

Cool Sun

Frozen ocean

Lakes in the frozen soil in summer

Layer of permanently frozen soil called permafrost

The Seasons and Weather

In regions such as the zone of tropical forest, the climate remains much the same throughout the year. But areas to the north and south of the equator experience seasonal changes – it is often much warmer in summer than in winter, and the summer months are generally drier. These changes are a result of the Earth being tilted in its orbit around the Sun. The Northern hemisphere is tilted closer to the Sun during its summer, while during the winter it is tilted away. For the Southern hemisphere the situation is reversed – its summer occurs when it is winter north of the equator.

But the weather in the temperate zone doesn't only change with the seasons. One day in summer it may be fine and sunny, the next, wet and cold. This is because two of the world's prevailing winds meet in this area – the warm Westerlies from the tropics and the cold Polar Easterly Winds. The lines along which these masses meet are called fronts, and it is here that variable and unsettled weather is experienced. These fronts move in bands around the globe, bringing different weather with them.

Just as in other climatic zones, the weather in the temperate zone is modified by land and sea effects. Both Edinburgh in Scotland and Moscow in the Soviet Union, for example, lie about the same distance to the north of the equator. But Moscow has much more severe winters and warmer summers, because it is located deep inside the Asian continental land mass. Edinburgh, on the other hand, lies on the coast and has weather that is notably milder than places a few kilometers farther inland.

Spring

Fall

Spring
During spring, the weather becomes warmer and the hours of daylight begin to increase. Seeds that have lain in the ground throughout the winter begin to sprout.

Summer
In summer the weather is at its warmest. The Sun is high in the sky and the most important winds affecting temperate climates at this time are those from the tropics.

Fall
The weather begins to cool in fall and the hours of daylight begin to shorten. Leaves fall from the trees, and seeds are produced from which next year's plants will grow.

Winter
In the winter the sun is low in the sky, and so its warmth has farther to travel through the atmosphere. Daylight hours are at their shortest during this season and the weather is usually cold.

Summer

Winter

The Seasons

The Earth circles, or "orbits" the Sun. A year is the time it takes to complete one full orbit. But the Earth also spins as it orbits – which is why we have day and night. The axis of this spin is an imaginary line running from the South pole to the North pole, through the Earth's center. This axis is tilted an angle of 23½° to the plane of its orbit. This means that at one period of the year the North pole faces the Sun, while six months later it is turned away from it. So at the poles it is continuous daylight for six months and continuous night for six months. People living in the extreme north of Europe and Canada experience the "midnight Sun" for only a few days.

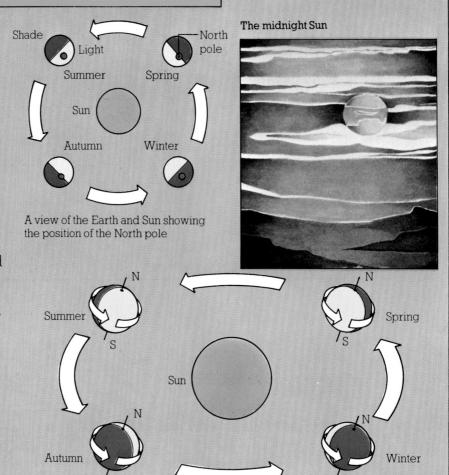

A view of the Earth and Sun showing the position of the North pole

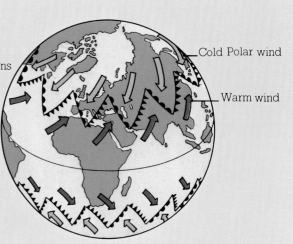

The midnight Sun

The Polar Fronts

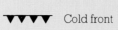

A weather map

Warm front

Cold front

Warm and cold fronts meet in temperate regions north and south of the equator

Equator

Cold Polar wind

Warm wind

●●●● Warm front

▼▼▼ Cold front

The meeting point of two global air masses is known as a front. There are two areas, one in Northern latitudes, the other in Southern latitudes, where warm masses of air from the tropics meet cold masses of air from the poles. The leading edge of a mass of cold air is called a cold front, that of warm air, a warm front. The way these air masses interact produces the variable weather found in regions of temperate climate.

Frontal Weather

In the Northern hemisphere, fronts always move eastward around the globe. When they meet, they begin to spiral around each other. This leads to a wedge of warm air being encircled by the colder air from the poles. Clouds form at the two fronts, and as one front passes over an area it often brings rain with it. Satellite photos show these fronts very clearly.

An aerial view of a frontal system

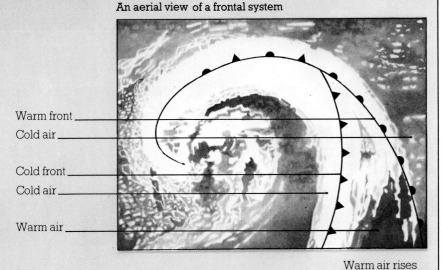

Warm front
Cold air
Cold front
Cold air
Warm air

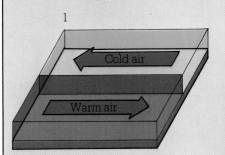

1

Warm air and cold air travel in opposite directions in temperate latitudes

Cold air
Warm air

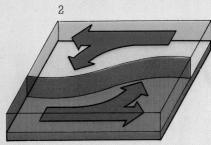

2

The warm and cold air masses begin to spiral around each other

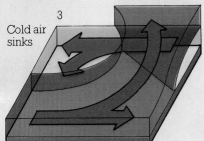

3

Cold air sinks

Warm air rises

Eventually the warm air rises above the cold

Mid-latitude weather

The masses of warm and cold air travel in opposing directions (1). The two fronts begin to spiral, and the warm air, being lighter, begins to rise above the cold (2). This causes the spiraling effect to increase, and the cold front moving in behind the mass of warm air begins to push it farther upward (3). As the warm front passes, the rising air lets its moisture fall as rain (4). Within the wedge of warm air, the weather remains stable for a while (5). At the cold front, the air rises very quickly and there may be heavy rain (6).

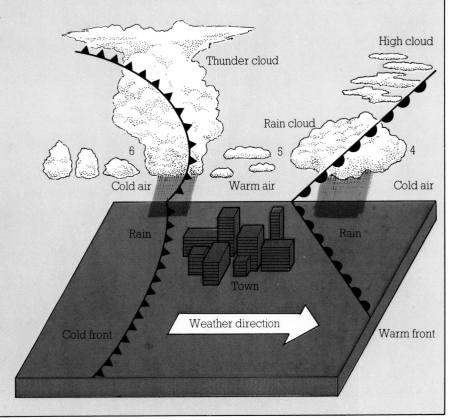

Thunder cloud

High cloud

Rain cloud

6

5

4

Cold air

Warm air

Cold air

Rain

Rain

Town

Cold front

Weather direction

Warm front

Clouds

All air – even that above the driest deserts – contains water. The vapor will only appear as clouds when it is at a certain concentration. This concentration depends upon the temperature of the air: warm air can hold much more water than cold air can before cloud formation takes place. Different kinds of cloud form at different heights, and each kind is associated with certain types of weather.

Cirrus
These are the highest clouds and are made of ice crystals. They are sometimes called mares' tails and often come before bad weather.

Altocumulus
Altocumulus is a medium-height cloud broken into regular lumps. It gives the "mackerel sky" that is often associated with fine weather.

Stratus
This forms an even layer of low cloud. The layer can be quite thin and it may cover hillsides. Drizzle often falls from it.

Stratocumulus
Stratocumulus cloud is quite similar to stratus, but tends to be thicker and contains dark rolls and shadows. It is found in a region of warm air.

Cumulus
Cumulus clouds have flat bases and well-defined, rounded tops. They are the typical "cotton wool" clouds and give rainy weather.

Cumulonimbus
The bases of these clouds are often low, but their anvil-shaped tops can reach 18,000 m (59,000 ft), where the water vapor freezes to ice. They form when warm air rises very quickly – when a cold front pushes up a mass of warm air, for example. The fierce updraughts of air in cumulonimbus often give rise to thunder and lightning and heavy rain and hail.

Snow, Rain and Hail

Clouds can release their moisture either as rain, snow or hail. Droplets of rain begin to form around small particles of ice or dust. When these droplets merge they eventually become large enough to fall as rain. Snowflakes form when the air temperature is below the freezing point of water – 0°C (32°F). This may occur either in winter or at high altitudes. Hail occurs when air rises rapidly as in a thunderstorm. Raindrops are lifted into freezing regions and become ice. This may happen many times until the drops fall as hail.

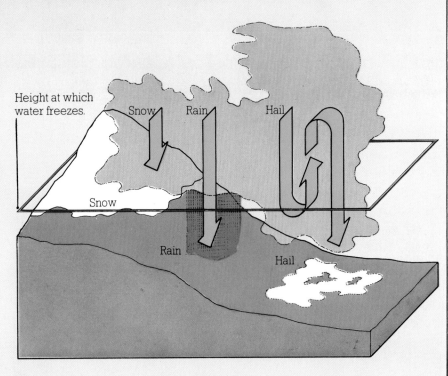

Height at which water freezes.

Snow

Rain

Hail

Snow

Rain

Hail

Meteorological Station

We can measure weather conditions by using different instruments. Thermometers can record maximum and minimum temperatures for a given period. A thermograph records how the temperature changes. The rain gauge collects rainwater so that the amount of rainfall can be measured. A hydrograph shows how the humidity – the air's dampness – changes. Wind speed and direction are measured by the anemometer's whirling cups. By taking these measurements, a picture of the changing weather in your given area can be built up.

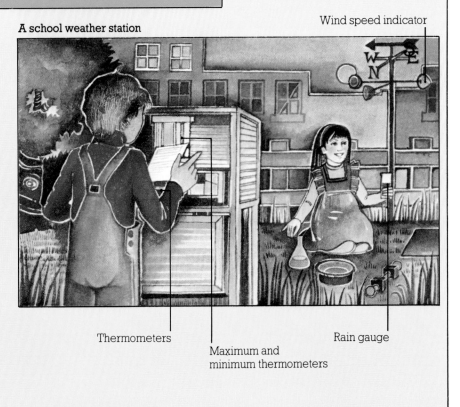

A school weather station

Wind speed indicator

Thermometers

Maximum and minimum thermometers

Rain gauge

Human Settlement

There is hardly any part of the globe in which people have not settled. In some cases, the settlement may be no bigger than one or two families and their livestock, in others the settlement may be a city as large as New York.

There is always a good reason for a settlement being where it is. If you look in the atlas, you will see that most of the world's major cities are located on an important river or on a coastline. This is because they grew up as trading centers, importing and exporting goods to serve their surrounding areas. Inland towns and cities are often at the meeting point of two or more land or river trading routes. With trade comes prosperity, so towns and cities can support increasing populations.

Agricultural settlements – farms and villages – need fertile soil and a supply of water for both crops and drinking. River valleys have both, and so are often densely settled – a large proportion of India's population, for example, lives in the plain of the Ganges River.

Another factor determining the siting of a settlement is that it can easily be defended against enemy attack in time of war. Many towns and villages were originally founded on hill sites for this reason.

The siting of new towns that have been built in this century is not so dependent on these factors. Many new towns are built to relieve overcrowding in major cities, and their siting may depend on local unemployment levels and the development of new industries.

▷ New York City is a classic route center site. For the last 300 years, people have been emigrating to North America from Europe, and New York has been the main port of entry. The city lies at the mouth of the Hudson River which provides a route through the Appalachian Mountains behind. The island site protected from the Atlantic Ocean by nearby Long Island was ideal for building docks. Since then, the granite rocks of the site have made ideal foundations for the city's skyscrapers.

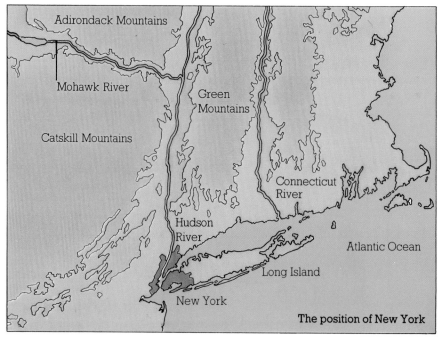

The position of New York

Populating America

North America is populated by peoples from all over the world. The American Indians came originally from Asia, during the last Ice Age. The Spanish arrived in the 15th century, and settled in the south west. The British and French took the East Coast and center. Africans and Indians came via the Caribbean. The Chinese population arrived as cheap labor during the expansion of America's West Coast.

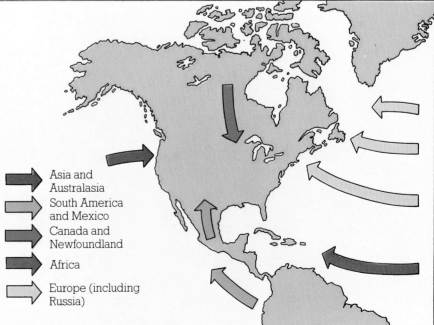

Asia and
Australasia

South America
and Mexico

Canada and
Newfoundland

Africa

Europe (including
Russia)

Defensible Site

From earliest times, human beings built their settlements in places that could be successfully defended against attack from neighboring tribes or armies. In those days, the main weapons were bows and arrows, and so a site on a hill, that could be surrounded by a high wall, was a good defensible place. Carcassonne in southern France, is a walled town built on a hillside in the early Middle Ages. It also lies on a route center, being where the valley of the River Aude opens out on to the plain. The main road from Narbonne to Toulouse runs nearby, as does an important canal. Today the old town of Carcassonne can still be seen, surrounded by its high walls. The modern town has now grown out beyond the old city walls.

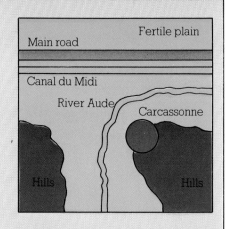

Carcassonne

Water Supply

An oasis

In desert areas the most precious thing is water. Towns in desert areas have always been sited where there is a good water supply The oasis towns of Algeria are a good example. Rain falls on the seaward side of the Atlas Mountains in northern Africa. It seeps underground into a layer of water-holding, permeable rock. When this layer reappears at the surface again – in this case in the Sahara Desert – the water forms small pools. Small towns and villages, called *oases*, grow up around these natural watering places.

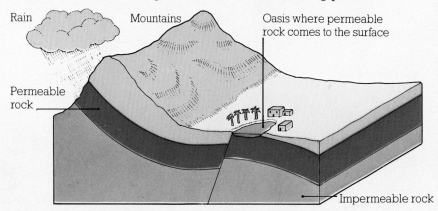

Industrial Sites

We often find manufacturing cities in areas where the raw materials of industry are to be found. To make steel we need iron. We also need coal to smelt it with. Both of these were found in south Wales and so a heavy engineering industry grew up there. Often these minerals were found and gathered on the surface. When this supply failed, mines were dug. The iron and the coal was found in the hills and valleys of this area and so towns grew along the valley floors, leaving upland farmland in between.

Industrial valley settlement

The towns stretch along the bottom of the valleys, squeezing in between the high hills.

Town growth along the valleys

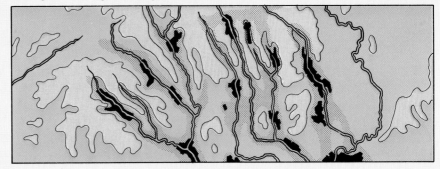

New Cities

Brasilia, the purpose-built capital of Brazil, is probably the most ambitious new city ever built. It is located in what was once thick tropical forest, and the buildings that house government offices have been designed in an ultra-modern style. Brasilia was inaugurated in 1960 and had no road or rail links, so goods and people had to be brought in by air. Appropriately enough, the city itself has an airliner-shaped outline. Unlike older settlements, new towns and cities are designed as a whole unit, with their full number of facilities such as schools and hospitals.

Brasilia

31

Mapping the Earth

The Earth from space

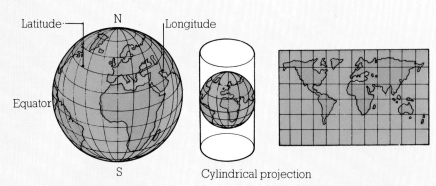

Latitude · Longitude

N

Equator

S

Cylindrical projection

People need maps for all sorts of reasons, and obviously the more accurate a map is the more useful it is. In reality, the Earth is a sphere slightly flattened at the top and bottom, and can be represented in a scaled-down version as a globe. Using lines of latitude that run parallel to the equator and lines of longitude that run through the poles, the position of any place can be pinpointed. The Earth's curved surface cannot be mapped on a flat sheet of paper with complete accuracy. Flat maps are made using *projections*. We pretend that a light bulb is placed at the center of the globe, casting shadows of the Earth's features onto a sheet of paper wrapped around it. The projection shown above is just one of many different types.

Scale

Using a map

Maps are made to many different scales. Large scale maps, showing details of individual buildings and footpaths are useful for exploring a small area on foot. Smaller scale maps may cover a whole country, showing major routes and geographical features. On a still smaller scale, a map may show a whole continent. Patterns of population distribution are often shown on such maps so that trends can be identified.

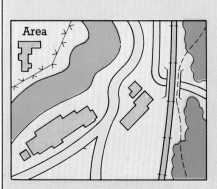

Area

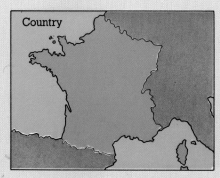

Country

Continent

Triangulation

Surveyor

To make an accurate map of an area surveyors use a method known as triangulation. First the surveyor measures a single straight line on the ground very accurately. This is the base line from which subsequent measurements are taken. The next stage is to draw imaginary lines from each end of the base line to the house or hill to be mapped. By measuring the angles between these lines and the base line, the surveyor can work out the distance to the house or hill. These new lines can be used as base lines themselves to map other features. Triangulation can also be used to measure height of hills and mountains. The base line is drawn horizontally to the ground. The angle between this and a line drawn to the summit is measured and from this the height can be calculated.

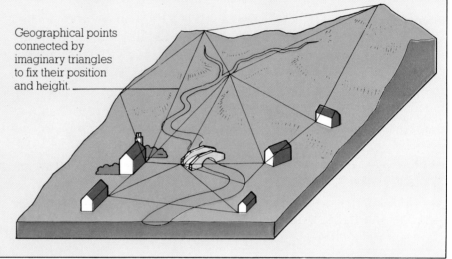

Geographical points connected by imaginary triangles to fix their position and height.

Relief

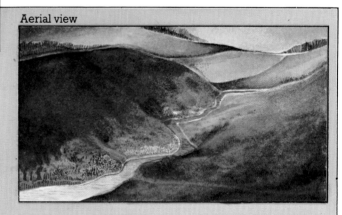

Aerial view

An aerial view of a hilly scene with a river running through it.

How can we show the different heights of hills and valleys on a flat map? One method is to use contour lines. These are lines that join up points that are the same height above sea level. On contour maps, the steeper the slope the more closely the contour lines are crowded together. Another method of showing height is to use color shading. Different shades of a color – usually brown – are used to indicate different levels of height. The highest areas are often shaded purple or white.

A contour – an imaginary line joining points of the same height.

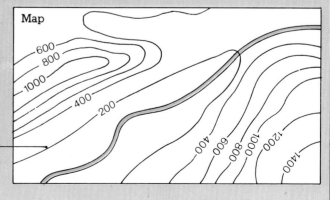

Map

Landscape Modification

When human beings changed from being hunters to become farmers, about 10,000 years ago, they began the process of changing the appearance of the Earth's surface. Since then, we have turned forests into farmlands, mined away at whole mountain sides, and dammed rivers to create huge artificial lakes.

The development of farming led to the establishment of cities – a farmer could produce more food than his family needed, so the surplus could be traded for other goods and services. People did not have to face the dangers of the natural world and populations began to expand.

After an initial period of expansion, population levels became relatively stable for many years, and the area of land under cultivation increased only slowly. It is only in the past thousand years or so that human beings have dramatically changed the landscape around them.

This period has seen the great forests that once covered northern Europe replaced by arable land. Industries have developed over the past 200 years, transforming places such as the Ruhr Valley in Germany. In the United States, vast tracts of wilderness have been placed under cultivation. Today, huge areas of tropical forest in Asia and South America are being cleared each day. These modifications often bring us great benefits, but they have their dangers, too. Over-farming can reduce the fertility of the soil, and when natural habitats are destroyed the animals living in them may face extinction.

Desert after irrigation

▷ At the beginning of the century, Imperial Valley in California was an arid desert. Since then the nearby Colorado River has been controlled by the Hoover Dam and the 130 km (81 miles) long All American Canal has been built to carry the water into the parched areas. Now a 4,800 km (2,983 miles) network of irrigation canals and ditches brings water to over 2,000 sq.km (1,200 sq. miles) of now fertile farmland. Crops of fruit are grown on an extensive scale where once there was only dry sand.

Desert before irrigation

Russian irrigation system

Many great rivers in the northern Soviet Union flow into the Arctic Ocean through semifrozen marshland. Their waters are of no use to anyone. During the late 1970s the Soviet Union proposed an ambitious plan to divert them southward to irrigate the desert areas in the south. The scheme has not gone ahead mainly because the shortage of water reaching the Arctic could affect the climate worldwide as well as locally.

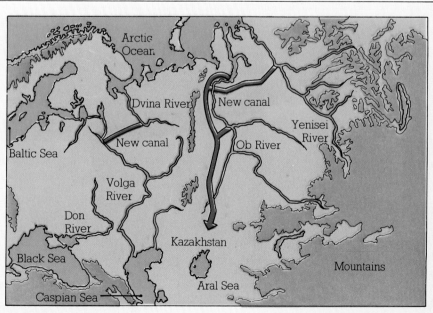

The Dust Bowl

Landscape modification isn't always for the best. In the 19th century the soil of the American Midwest was heavily tilled by settlers. Gradually the soil dried out and broke down into dust. In 1934 strong winds lifted a dustcloud that covered nearly two-thirds of the United States and stripped the soil of the four "dust bowl" states of Kansas, Oklahoma, Texas and Colorado. It became impossible to grow anything in the soil that was left and thousands of farms were ruined. Even today, farming in many parts of these regions is poor.

An abandoned farm in the Midwest of the USA

Man-made Deserts

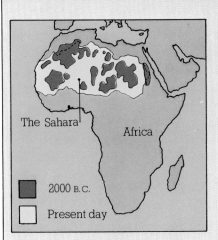

The Sahara

Africa

2000 B.C.

Present day

The Sahara Desert

Four thousand years ago, the Sahara Desert occupied isolated patches surrounded by grasslands. It grew as local herdsmen allowed too many cattle to graze on the grasses. The grass did not have time to grow again and the land soon became too poor to support cattle. Grazing by sheep and goats continued the deterioration. When the grass disappeared there were no roots to bind the soil together and the area became desert. Today there is an area south of the Sahara called the Sahel. Over-grazing and drought are turning these grasslands into desert.

Destroying Tropical Forests

Tropical forests can also suffer from thoughtless farming. Tropical forests are slashed down and burnt to create clearings. Crops grown in the clearings rapidly remove essential nutrients from the soil, so that after a year or so it becomes barren. The farmers then move on to clear another area. The forest has no time to re-establish itself before the soil breaks down and is washed or blown away.

Cattle ranch in Brazil

Making New Land

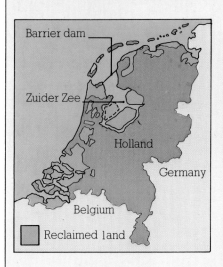
Barrier dam
Zuider Zee
Holland
Germany
Belgium
Reclaimed land

Farms on the Dutch Polders

The Dutch people are experts at producing new land. During the first century A.D. the coastline of the Netherlands was submerged by a rising sea level. People who lived there at the time built the first high walls, called dikes, to keep back the high tides. Since the Middle Ages, the Dutch have been building dikes to enclose sheltered areas of water in shallow coastal lagoons, and pumped out the water. The reclaimed areas are called polders and many of them date from the 15th century. In the 1920s a large dam was built across the Zuider Zee to turn it into a freshwater lake. The lake was divided up by dikes and each division was pumped out. These reclaimed areas are all below sea level and any water seeping in has to be pumped out all the time to prevent flooding. About a quarter of the land area of the Netherlands has been reclaimed from the sea in this manner.

Glossary

Alluvium   This is the sand, gravel, clay and other eroded material deposited by a river.

Atmosphere   The thin layer of gases that surrounds the Earth.

Atoll   A circular or horseshoe-shaped coral island.

Climate   The typical weather of a place, based on the average conditions noted over a period of years.

Continent   A large land mass. The world's continents are North America, South America, Africa, Asia, Europe, Oceania and Antarctica.

Equator   An imaginary circular line dividing the Earth into Northern and Southern hemispheres.

Erosion   The wearing away of the Earth's surface by the action of weather, rivers, glaciers and the sea.

Front   The line at which masses of air of different temperatures meet.

Glacier   A mass of ice, formed of compressed snow, found in mountains and cold climates.

Groundwater   Water that seeps through the soil and rocks of the Earth's surface.

Irrigation   The process of bringing water to a dry area to enable crops to be grown.

Latitude   Parallel lines of latitude are drawn to the north and south of the equator. With the lines of longitude (see below) they are used to pinpoint the position of a place on the Earth's surface.

Longitude   Lines of longitude are drawn through the North and South poles. Distances are measured east and west of the line of longitude that passes through Greenwich in London.

Moraine   The material carried and deposited by glaciers.

Permeable rock   Rock through which water can pass – limestone, for example. Rocks which don't allow water through them are called impermeable.

Projection   The method used to represent a curved surface, such as the Earth's, on a flat piece of paper.

Tropics   The tropics of Cancer and Capricorn are two imaginary lines drawn north and south of the equator. The area between these lines is called the tropics. The Sun is directly overhead here at some part of the year.

Water table   The upper surface of that region of the ground that is saturated with water.

Water vapor   The invisible moisture in the air. It condenses to form clouds and fogs.

Weathering   The decay and breaking up of surface rocks that precedes erosion.

Index

PRINTED IN BELGIUM BY

proost

INTERNATIONAL BOOK PRODUCTION